MW00583231

David Keplinger

The Most
Natural Thing

New Issues Poetry & Prose

A Green Rose Book

New Issues Poetry & Prose
The College of Arts and Sciences
Western Michigan University
Kalamazoo, Michigan 49008

First Edition, 2013.

ISBN: 978-1-936970-15-5 (paperbound)

Library of Congress Cataloging-in-Publication Data:
Keplinger, David.
The Most Natural Thing/David Keplinger
Library of Congress Control Number: 2012940515

Editor:	William Olsen
Managing Editor:	Kimberly Kolbe
Layout Editor:	Elizabyth A. Hiscox
Assistant Editor:	Traci Brimhall
Art Director:	Christopher Fox
Designer:	Christopher Kurtz
Production:	Paul Sizer
	The Design Center, Frostic School of Art
	College of Fine Arts
	Western Michigan University
Printing:	McNaughton & Gunn, Inc.

The Most Natural Thing

David Keplinger

New Issues

WESTERN MICHIGAN UNIVERSITY

Also by David Keplinger

The Rose Inside

The Clearing

The Prayers of Others

World Cut Out with Crooked Scissors: The Selected Poetry of
  Carsten René Nielson
  (Translation)

House Inspections
  (Translation of prose poems by Carsten René Nielsen)

By and By: The Copybook Songs of Isaac P. Anderson
  (Multi-Media)

To Annette and Daniel

Contents

What is this enigmatic impulse that does not allow one to settle down in the achieved, the finished? I think it is a quest for reality.

—Czeslaw Milosz

Incision

Enormous Yellow Sky

The same as everyone, I hunted for mushrooms before I was born, under the two dimensional plane of the sky. These were the woods where one meets the deer, the goddess in disguise. Her symbol: what's hidden would like to be known. She led me to a banquet in the clearing. Several guests sat talking at a long table. "Soon no one alive will remember the eighteenth century," whispers my father into my mother's ear. "One day this too will be a fairy tale," says my mother from behind her carnival mask.

The Assumption

From its pellet-like source, the universe widens. Our car broke down near the fairgrounds that winter. There I once saw the World's Tallest Man, harrowed by his ankylosis, his knees like liquidy magic eight balls. He sat in a chair waving at us. Then he rose as if climbing a rope. Five o'clock, just about dark. The tow truck arrived. It cranked down its hook on a chain. It hoisted the bumper, lip of a fish, almost vertical. All together we climbed in the truck. The father, the son, the quiet driver.

Almost, Not Quite There

On its outer discs the rods shift light into a message in the brain. They work on the periphery, function best in dark. My father wakes from sleep and asks, *Where are we, Davey?* He's going blind this year. The rods are master translators, but their work is imprecise. The road is slick, covered in black leaves. Deer leap over headlights like white fences in the foreground. I, the deer, my father, briefly exist in three realities, separate in outcome. But any moment now he'll see the deer, gasp his tiny breath.

In Translation: 1901

Her nickname will be Little Bread, after the bread she brings for lunch. First day of school, she comes without English, as though the dog ate it. Teacher asks her name. She holds up her lunch, a little bread. Which makes them laugh. She pokes two eyes in that roll, folds the bald dolly into her napkin, stuffs it in her coat. It's plain to everyone, shaking their heads: she came unprepared for the twentieth century. You can tell by the sepia tone in her skin. Her hair is so tangled it will have to be shaved.

"My Heart Swims in Blood"

Stone steps lead to the water and the steps go down and
in. The master builder made it so these stairs continue
farther, farther into the Loire, climbed by fish and grazed
in lightness by the feet of swimmers. The ruling body
planted chestnuts here. Forest chestnuts grew, fell, and
hollowed out. No new trees replaced them. To clear the
song out of my head I swim out of the shallows as light
that shines through chestnut leaves falls in patches of
huge brightness—but under water I hear just one thing.

Slowness

The slow boy bats his swimming hands out in the reservoir. His mother, slow to admit his impediments, has let him go too deep, and he lunges, sucked into her egg of light. I've been a peasant all my life. I rip the bread. I eat too fast. I rush the prayer at table. In this frame before his drowning, the universe is slow, and I want to be fast. The mother shows her worry now. She lifts her hand, cups it over the sun. The swimmer bats in furious wheels but gets no closer, embarrassed by this slowness he is learning.

Take Messina

You'd be impressed and even sad that I remember. The crag of mottled rocks suggesting faces like the toothless pensioners. In Messina you're alone, available, the youth still rising in your cheek. As if there'll be no end to youth and solitude, the sea below Messina answers: *solitude is beauty*, but you grow cold, walk back to the hotel, and light begins to change, at each stage resonant. Messina? I have never been. You told the story quickly when I loved you. Now here it is exactly as you left it, these faces old, or like children, elated by a missing tooth.

The Herd Gate Injury

The herd gate didn't tear the shoulder from the neck, it tore the neck from the shoulder, and the neck was displaced in far-flung angles. To the feedlot they carried this man, who was quiet the entire way. He held his hand against the neck. He did it to keep it from falling off the spinning world. Which is to say, he did it to keep it from falling off his body. The feedlot doors stood like a hangar. I'll pay for the gate, he finally said. In careful English. I'll pay for everything I did and I am very sorry.

Aloysius Bertrand

Something in the grass is moving, but so small I can barely make it out. Maybe it's the poet Aloysius Bertrand, whom history has turned into a toad. When I bend to the grass to try to see, the blades of grass separate like the curtain of a puppet theater. No, they open like the spine of a book untouched for centuries. No, they're blades of grass. I hear a story coming from an amphibious voice. A buck-toothed girl once tried to kiss a toad, but it had always been a toad. So nothing happened.

Hair

I sit at her feet with a razor, she stands right above me, her crotch smeared with cream, her face in the mirror, laughing, the black hair still coating her back and her shoulders. We start with the thinnest of hair, and Anicka shaves the soft wisps from her nipples—: I slough off the scuzz from my nape; buzz cut my head; she plucks off her eyebrows. We could go farther. There's always more to cut. We cut from the pores of the arms and the crawl space of the nostril (to know where everything is hidden).

The Dead in Certain Old Photographs

The rich at Fleury are covered in flowers; the servants lie tangled in oak tree roots. So it is discovered when one mound is dug up, using shovels and picks and the flash of yellow sepia. At this exhumation, it is 1920. The modern swimmers watch unselfconscious in bloomers and high-fitting trunks, drinking young wine from flutes and talking, laughing, shushing each other. The one whose name is Asa, not from this country, falls backwards in the water. As she does this, her hair fans into a brown corona.

The Jaw

You must hit to the jaw, my father says. I know his hands ache in their taping, and mine do, too. As a young man in a bar in Barcelona he was hit from behind with a bottle and fell into his attacker's arms, who cut him in the face. We must hit to the jaw, he says, and when it's my turn the bag is still swaying. He's seventy three years old. He holds his hands in protection, up high. He's filled with these crazy expressions: Hit to the jaw. Keep up your guard. Punch hard, once. Don't think you have forever.

Exiting the Room Backwards While Bowing Deeply from the Waist

If you judge me at the end, remember, please, all the details of what happened. The painter Lorenzetti hung me tangled in the palsied branches of a fig tree, where the straight line of rope would hurt most. Dante nailed me to the floor of hell. But all you moderns crucified me, hung me from your telephone poles, televised my execution. Now my belly aches. It swirls in the whoosh of blue-green urges. I walk around sleepy. My eyes are shut. You can blame me for everything. But give me a boxer's face.

Who as Subject, Whom as Object

For the second week in spring before it spoils, the little
huts are warm at Valley Forge. Puckering trout crowd up
the shallows of the Brandywine. Something has returned,
it's safe to say, to give birth to the world again. The
Hessian ghost will brave the light in emerald wool. In
repose like happy Buddhas are the pellets in his musket.
In his head, his death-day is still dragoon blue. His
home's this church, its owl in the roof, its Christ on the
rood. The one is lunging hungrily—and one is letting go.

Whatever Sings Belongs to No One

Our singing girl turns three, sings to herself, blows the candles by herself. Whatever sings belongs to no one, she still knows, so sing, the idea is to sing, keep singing, then never let them make you stop. Does she already hear the peripheral doubts, does she see us yet, the terror figures she'll become? She wants to flee us in her minuscule car, singing, the cast from last month's accident already too small for her hand. She waves three fingers through that cast. I see a wolf mouth, swallowing the tail of a bird.

For Danielle Meals

The Sockets

We played Flash Gordon. The Martians wore black
helmets shaped like widow's peaks. They never wanted
to fight. In their clubhouse, made up like the red hills of
Mars, they drank from long flutes of glacier ices—milk,
actually. We attacked and there sat the King, a fat boy
whose eyes were unnaturally shadowed. "You look like
French Astronauts!" He said of our tights. His mother
spent years in the mental ward. It was his eyes that made
us draw back—the depth of their sockets, the being seen.

The French Symbolists

Rimbaud left Harare, the disease in his knee, in his groin, in his gut soaring upward like a moth toward something lit inside him. He sought the way home on an elephant. Knock-kneed, the elephant stomped toward Algiers. Still the gray moth kept rising toward the bulb of the spleen. The spleen, from underuse, had gotten so hot it began to dissolve into ashes. At the spleen's flashpoint the elephant, Rimbaud, and the cancer achieved weightlessness. None of the hooves touched the ground.

In Translation: Sperm

Candy Bright resembled her own name, her breath of
cookie-breakfasts saying things. In one filmstrip frantic
sperm rivaled upward toward the egg: I took them to be
tadpoles, each life a panicked tailfin, a giant head. How
difficult to see things as they are. On the quiz that
followed, *tadpole* was the word I wrote. Leave it to
myself to love the metaphor; forget the thing: That
desperate, translucent half-a-self, said Candy Bright, was
sperm, her whisper crisp, a spark spit out from the forge.

Capillaries

From farther and farther away, my mother's voice grows
louder in the memory. I may be suckling her breast; then
I'm running through a fire-bombed city. Blood pours
through the neighborhoods in capillaries. I hear the voice
much louder than the mortar fire. It's in the language of
attackers, made of bullets and money. You're all that's
left on earth, the voice is shouting. You have made one
thoughtless error. You'll have to stoop to enter heaven.
Look at you, you're Krishna, dressed in perfect weather.

The Tongue

Raw oysters sleep a vampire sleep and their coffin beds gleam. I chug and snuffle up the meat. Anicka holds one monster to her lips and can't stop laughing, squinching up her face. All brine and cold it floats in front of her mouth. We're exiles again, we're in Prague again, so I recite Tsvetaeva's "and soon we all will sleep beneath the earth . . . " Anicka tips her oyster into place and sucks back hard. Her eyes are closed. She dabs her chin with my enormous red tie. I sit here helpless as she's licked by it.

Cilia

I am taken to surgery, they say cancer in my lung. The surgeon is Anicka, eyes smiling behind her mask. Then I dissolve in the loam of sleep. She discovers a tree she calls a *smrk,* branching upward in the darkness of my windpipe. She must give the tree back like a gift: uprooted, it sits on the tip of her finger. To grow a *smrk,* the lung must be tar-sore and black, well soiled. In Czech the word for death is *smrt.* Not the tree, but how the "t" moves back into Anicka's mouth, is the miraculous thing.

Vasco De Gama Rounds the Horn

Mrs. Malvina bent from the waist. De Gama broke through to the East, she said, as round The Horn she scraped her chalk. When she stood up, the chalk had marked her black dress. From the back of my head came De Gama's white sails, and it was thus that he became my horror: I dreamt of him for years, his steel-fingered gloves. The sultan welcomed him in Mozambique. He looted in Mombasa. The treasure was enormous, Malvina said. And she brushed her slight belly with her hands.

In Translation: Mercury

I made good money when I was 16. I bussed for Joanne who'd just turned 30, and she touched my hand at the ice machine. We smoked clove cigarettes. We took a long ride into Hatfield and the packaging smell. Our drinks in fat casino cups, I drove her Mercury. On the passenger side she opened her work shirt. She loosened the bra from one shoulder. I pulled into a row of corn, leaned over, swaying like a suicide. Change was pouring from my pockets. Suck harder, she said. You could get a little milk.

Shadow Puppets in a Black Box Theater

On the X-ray of my lung the doctor discovers a node: a calcified region of scar. At one end it's widening, at the other diminishing, fading into grayish effervescence. With his finger he traces a line from the flute toward the widening bulb. He points to that bulb, as if trying to jam just one finger into its opening. Bafflement, his diagnosis—no blue sarcoma in my skin. I've never sandblasted stone. No silico-tuberculosis. No reason to be there at all. I have no reason for a keyhole in my lung.

"Winter Landscape with a Bird Catch"

Medieval children standing up on metal curlicues, skating a river of scudded ice. Where roots of oaks burst from the riverbank, the village ends. From a limb two crows are watching as they oversee the laws. No one is to cross those oaks. No one is to speak about the cold. There's a man who resembles me here, so I ask, is this really the pinnacle, is this the peak of a forty-year life? Breughel has painted his horrible answer: he bends to look more closely at, set under the ice, what appears to be an infant's head.

On Seeing the Ravennan Mosaics

On a wall inside the San Vitale you can find a little boat embarking, come from the age of Justinian. The hull is made of gold. Embarking toward nowhere, forever. The boat is the size, almost, of a hand held iron, the one my mother would depress into my father's white handkerchiefs. I tried to touch the iron. I wanted it to steam at the test of my wet finger. Of course, I was forbidden to. When I tried to touch the wall inside the San Vitale, to make it steam, my efforts had little effect. I stood on tiptoes. I could reach it—nearly. But it was too high up, as always.

Manipulation

A Comedy in Three Acts

When you set my life story to music, use triadic structures like the one four five. Every detail of the story should be set in threes. Three trees are split by lightning on my death day; the same trees that were planted at my birth. The midwife slaps three times. I breathe three dying breaths. On the eve of my conception, my mother takes three sips from her first Napoleon Brandy. Near Tripoli, my father fires at steel gray sharks, three shots at a time, now teetering from the ledge of his battleship.

Ostrava in the Afterlife

The whitewashed agencies, calm offices: no trouble from the
boys who once graffitied there, "Jan Pallach Burns for This."
The sky is clear but miners' faces, now retired, darken from
the booze. The students vacate their parents' shoebox
tenements. On Janackova I shared one myself with sore-
throated neighbors in slippers, their furies reaching through
the plaster walls. Their TVs spoke softly the news. I
remember a commercial from back then, a voice like a
cartoon mouse's, selling tissues into which he cried.

A Play about the Way Words Taste

In the play there is no dialogue. Just recipes. A man and woman sit eating soup. The soup is fine until a waiter tells the woman what she's eating. The man sits frowning, saying, "Tripe! Marjoram! Garlic! Ham!" as if to say, *Eat it! Let's not cause a scene,* his coffee spoon about to touch the surface of the coffee, her soup spoon lifting tripe into her face. The waiter is about to suggest another dish entirely. Her lips are pursed. The soup hangs suspended. Her eyes are half closed, or just now opening.

Alpine Scratchings on the EKG

Here is a model heart, giant size, held near my doctor's
face, his Valentine. Blue cords ravel inward to the
labyrinthine chambers where the ventricles contract. All
my fantasies reveal I'm strong, I'm aging well, enjoying
my vitality, like an elderly Swiss, laughing, batting at the
asses of my Dobermans. My doctor is a good man, good
at what he tries to do. He has bad news, but smiles into
his Valentine. Never mind this heart—he seems to say—
this head of the Minotaur—dead, in Theseus' hands.

The Right Brain

To activate it, strict codes of conduct were applied. John Keats wore ruffles and a jacket, slacks with a ribbon of satin, hemmed to his size. There's Emily's gown, apocryphal, bleached, and Blake's scratched boots, his feet dunked in them. There's Hart Crane's weird drinking blouse; the collar wound with an ascot; the cloak and headscarf of Marianne Moore; Pound's shabby trousers, the fly is down. It's Saturday evening. They've had their baths. They dress themselves in these uniforms. For this.

A Day at Olesna

We are right here. We are in this water. From the water I
lift up my hand; up shoots that vague sense of being in
time, of being here always, of waiting for my hand to rise
and for my mind to look at it. I ask myself, can all that's
happened have been real? Then, Anicka, your hair pulled
back into a ponytail, which floats spread out, feathered,
on the lake, you undo the thin string of your top. At last
we are right here. The water beads against my hand. You
wave your top in the air like a flag. Your ribs slip under.

The Belly

I fell into my mother's purse, and out shut the world with
a snap. There I lay, coming to, among her tubes of
lipstick, box of Chiclets, leather gloves. Death smelled
of mint and a decolleté of *Charlie*. No crow was going to
come to peck the artery of this whale and free me from
my loneliness, snapped up tight, with very little air to last
me. It was a feeling of such power (I was a special child)
I'm afraid it got the best of me. I made a throne out of the
compact puff. I ruled by my scepter, an unlit match.

The Heart

The morning before his open-heart surgery my father and
I drive to Elmwood Park Zoo. But no one greets us at the
gate. The stalls for the animals are suddenly gone, the
zoo defunct. I think of the giraffes somewhere munching
on trees, feeding on anything that will not scream. I think
of the lion, gorged in the woods, how his meat, until now,
has never been heart. In the forests rise weeds, a messy
world of unseparate things. Raptors above us. Big cats
mewl. Mounds of apes wake up amazed, no cages.

The Bladder

He who'll lose his bladder calls it Three Days Down, or The Haunted Mere. It must be reconstructed from other body parts. I imagine what those parts will be, elastic like the wrist, thin like the skin where the cheek meets the tragus of the ear. Small mushrooms have begun to grow along the inner lining of the bag. Doctors scrape the lining; but then, the mushrooms again. You would have to swim into that lake, he says, not breathe for days, to kill its monster. That's how he talks. That's the only way.

The Night We Stayed at the Whitehorse Flophouse

I had so little money, I stiffed our Indian waiter.
Followed by a herd of busboys he played the fipple for
Anicka anyway, plummeting registers in glissando. To
his lips he held the pipe; his lips were pursed in her
direction. I was Krishna the troublemaker, she said. He
was the shepherd Krishna. The flophouse was next door.
The concierge was reading a newspaper. At each turn of
a page he wet his finger with his lips. Our room was a
closet the length of our bodies, a tablecloth for a sheet.

Appendix

Is it my end or my beginning? The appendix began in my grass-eating time. It craves the cud the dawn horse chewed, and the buffalo herds in the oceans of plains, and the giraffe whose mouth hoards a muscle so enormous, it must be kept at great distance from the heart. But the appendix began before all that, even before the grass eating time. It began as primordial cell: hungry, an inner sun that craved the outer one. Now it floats, a post-script to itself, a large bloated tongue in the viscera.

The Fetal Position

There's mulleted, acned, good-as-dead Rick, pumping
gas into his Chopper, the way we knew him last. We hated
him. We all grew up; he fell into the Bergey Mill ditch
and stayed sixteen. At the pump he sucked out smoke
from the butt of a clove. I said something to the tune of,
"That thing taste good enough to blow us up?" He just
spit into his fingertips, doused the cigarette, flicked it to
me laughing. Good-as-dead Rick. One breath of smoke
kept exhaling at my feet: crumpled, grimy, hot, and wet.

The Larynx

Let my grandfather eat in his silence again, except for the scrape of his fork. Let him make a little sound when food rains through the laryngectomy. Let him spin a column of spaghetti and chew slowly, filling himself until he's fat. Wide and fat. Let him pluck sardines and chew their bones inside his mouth. Who am I to say? I'll ask no questions of my grandfather. My grandfather asks no questions of me. This meal is finished. And with that, with that weight, let him push from the head of the table.

Idiom

The mule went blind and we were destitute. By day it kept knocking its skull into trees. It had to wear a head bandage. It would curl up to my mother in her sleep, kick her at night. Its tubular hooves would not cease galloping toward some far off Jerusalem. My grandfather played the encouraging poet. "Never throw your guns into the field," he said. Just then, a snowstorm befell us. My family needed half a buttock for the Christmas feast. What a world that was. I was asleep in the manger.

The Kidney

Prospector's tin, the kidney has found gold. That stone is pebble-round, an incandescence. The kidney stone is heaviest when passing through the tubes and channels of the body, falling, ineluctably falling. Through restless, hypertensive sleep, I've felt the kidney ticking like my hips are taped with bombs. I've anointed it with bourbon, gold made out of corn. I knew a man who was shot in the kidney. He began to speak in strange tongues—untranslating blues—but died from the song.

In Translation: Nevermore

The crow is a *ptak*, which also means a pencil dick, which means a useless tool. The crow of the poet they love says *nekrat zase*, nevermore, in the *kraaa* of its slavik tongue always. I ask them in English one morning while it is still dark, inspired by a field set with crows. What does the crow say here? It's eight seventeen, says the clock. *Kra*, together they say. I remember the clean antique shops in Frydek, lit by stripes of dusty light, a service tray set with a flask and four glasses: each with the star still on them.

Story Is

There's no way to describe this thing. The headless body wants to take flight, escape its bad death, it still has a chance, thinking pouring from the bloody spout. The head kind of watched as the body flew off. I threw down my hatchet and then lost sight of it. I found it under the henhouse run—true story!—where it was born. The body had a raptor's heart. It scuttled upwards on its tippy toes, like trying to leap to its head—to soar back inside it—which you or I would do, story is, by swimming with our hands.

Late August, Germanesque

Cicada, also, starts from underground. It opens its
enormous sideways eyes. It struggles upward towards its
death, which is its song. Today I passed a man-sized tree,
just my height, flowering with almost-deadness. On its
coffin-boat, which was a brittle leaf, cicada returned my
stare. Its eye wound round and round. It starts from
underground. A part of me could crawl up out of me,
forget myself, and sing. A person can go years, cleaning
ashes from the fireplace. You look again, they shine.

The Crown of Light at Assisi

San Damiano, I am told, has been repaired, a marvel at
the bottom of this hill. Against the bicep-width of
olive trunk I watched a blade of grass a school of tiny
snails were climbing. Their footfalls were lighter than air.
I have been ready for a change, after all this preparation.
Then I'm told, "One must be shattered, then repaired
through one's desire to know God." The blade hardly bent
beneath that weight. I'm a blade of grass, a waving spine.
The hollow brain up at the top. The heart is alive, in tow.

At the Hermitage small yellow insects, half butterfly, half
bee, land on my notebook, fall from trees in rain. No one
speaks of them. They cover the words, "the happiest me."
Even the nib of ink from my pen, they lick from the paper.
I've made a list: First, your acts of kindness, then the
parents you forgave, then the eyes you healed, the ears,
then leprosies, then how you learned to speak to birds, and
every flying thing, calling them to hear you teach them
nothing, assuring them with quiet gestures of the hand.

*

Where Giotto got the urge to paint God's finger, only the tip of the finger, poked through narrow clouds, I hear a voice in baritone, just over there. The voice gets loud, and as quickly, stops. Mr. Old Man in the window with his eyes keeps following: What am I doing on this road without a festival in tow? He waves, but only a finger. Go there, the finger says, and then retracts. I follow it to where I hear again: the baritone voice from dimensionless space; I see the door that it is singing from, flung open.

*

On her sarcophagus, Calvetta's head is flanked on one side by a pine cone; on the other by a robin. Beautiful things are coming to term and some do not survive, the servants of the words have been saying. I am a servant of that wisdom, and I believe them. Calvetta lived her twenty years on this Umbrian hill. Her face, no expression, beside the pine cone's pagoda. She had her stone-like body two millennia ago. A pine cone is much lighter than the body. A robin is much lighter than the body. These nice ideas don't console me.

*

Your limestone pillow shined by faces: those who slept here after yours did. Your cave was cut out with a pick. But I don't believe in that story. I want some proof, I want to take a picture, I want to say things with authority. Which is to say, I want to be assured that I will live. The lens doesn't care what I want. Rain, the slime and green of living stone, and an image enters in. I seek an instrument, the slime and rain are saying. Whatever you desired in your authoring, the stone bed says, rest here.

Removal

Eyelids in the Dawn Years of Perspective

Time kept passing and I wasn't getting born. My parents
called for me. They made me a room, erected a tiny straw
bed. Greece fell and shattered into tiny bits; then Rome
took a broom to the world. It was passing before I could
open my eyes—my eyelids so thin I could see
apparitions, figures floating just beyond the scrim.
Suddenly, Breughel the Elder lifted a brush—tilting his
horny, drunk dancers. At that point the day and the night
slammed together: which locked me in their forceps hold.

"An Insistent and Eager Harmoniousness to Things"

Like an enormous leech the pancreas lies with its head tucked into the duodenum, upside down, the tail outstretched over it, an animal curled in on itself. In the preserve jar of the belly, it wriggles like a strange, medieval cure. When we sleep, Anicka, the pancreas secretes its juices, reverting tonight's *toutlerre* into Germanic syllables again: *cake, meat, blood.* All of this healing is out of our hands. I turn to you, completely unconscious. Completely unconscious, you turn to me.

Sleepwalking

As I reveal myself to the world, the world will be revealed to me. My father used to sleepwalk, hammering invisible nails into the walls of the house. Then his invisible hammer would land on his thumb. He held the skin, it beat with pain. To wake him up, I'd have to learn to speak in signs, practice the agony's grammar. I'd gently take the hammer from his hands. Waking he would see there was no hammer, no nail. No thumb. No skin. No sleeping. No waking. No need of saving.

Anatomy of a Skeleton

I see Anicka in a bone-white pool, dog-paddling, when I'm finally gone. I see there will be better books to read, husky cops will come to check on her. She'll live where people leap from burning towers onto trampolines and fall into the arms of lovers. She's absolutely free, light as a skeleton, swimming around the lip of the pool, then stopping when she's tired to sip a green, umbrellaed drink. A fireman. A cop. I eat up my fantasy—three or four portions per night. But it never puts fat on my bones.

Punishment

There stood a birch his father planted the year my father was born. The American Birch grows no arms while it's a sapling. In 1939, my father almost killed this birch, snapping off, in pride or affection, the first branch from the tree. His father beat him with that very branch! But it survived, he brought me there, we stood under it. This is why some icons can reduce me to tears. This is why I flinch at contact with the Eucharist. Along the trunk, no branches, very little shadow. Uppermost, a coronation.

The Unicorn in Modern Memory

The unicorn was just a dumb rhinoceros, authorities are saying now. But I don't believe it. The rhino is covered by plates like hard plaque, but unicorn, I once heard, was the most sought after prey, always fleeing through the woods of our primeval memory. How does one resolve this contradiction? I believe my grandmother wanted to tell me. This was as she rose to leave the house, in the middle of the night. And with no warning in particular, her singing voice transformed into an Alzheimer's sigh.

Action

Balanced on your uncle's shoe you hold his hand like a
balloon, his sideways buckle clamped above the left-hand
thigh, buttered in a flashbulb's bright. Everyone who sees
this picture says: so happy, so active is the little girl. But
you remember those years differently. It's Christmastime.
Your mother is inside, hanging ornaments, fake candy canes,
false beards and clouds. Dirt road, wet with snow—and
now you step down from the pointed shoe, decisively—
and he is just about to, but doesn't let go of your hand.

In Translation: Woe-mood

A word in this language, *Vemod,* woe-mood, has no English counterpart. Anicka is describing her father's last gasp—*huhp* she says, breathing in quickly. "He was enveloped by our *vemod,*" she says. His writing desk stands in the background, inert, its oak slab stuck out like a tongue, for show. It has a blotter, there's some writing still depressed in it, as though the blotter sucked the words back in. "An image, however Godlike, is not God," it will reveal in the rubbing she'll shush over it.

Near the Amphitheater at Gubbio

Along the *via regia,* a woman at the café-bar seduced a
man. He was much younger. His hair was combed high,
unfashionably. The woman pushed it down with her
hand. They'd drunk a lot. She wet her fingers at her lips.
So much is happening in secret, right before our eyes.
Along the ruined *via regia,* there was a hush like the start
of a play. We were its audience, breathing a breath. The
young man reached to pay for the bill. The woman,
whispering something, poured him the last of the wine.

The Sleepers

I am running under trees and clouds, this is how I see my life. But sometimes I touch Anicka's collarbone along the fissure, an old accident. Two kilometers from Krasna, we sleep like that, in her dead grandmother's bed, my hand resting softly on her once broken shoulder. It is the room her mother made for us. Her parents, too, step into their massive wooden beds. Then moon pours through the window on our bones. Gardenias painted on the walls. Death's white calmness. A room that has filled up with sheep.

"May I See What You Are"

I was waiting for what stirred inside the reeds to stir again, when I asked: *May I see what you are,* and quieted myself, felt my heart clank like a cup inside, up and down the cell bars of the ribs. But nothing moved. I thought about the day reprieves won't come, despite my having other plans; how I would beg but lose myself; lose you, Anicka; an apocalypse. A wave smashed up against the shore. Then in the reeds the stork began to flush and—*now see what I am?*—open its colossal wings.

Fat

Save everything, throw away nothing, my people taught me, and that's why my home is all mismatching silver, all mirrors and discordant furniture. This TV used to be my grandmother's. It's still warming up, tuned to the channel with cowboy shows playing. On the radio clock it is three a.m. Her fattening spirit gets up in the dark, does its chores in the dark to her shows. Today it's Tex Ritter. *Goodbye my little Cherokee,* he sings to my grandmother, who bows as she tips down her percolator.

Gender Study

I came down with a deathly flu and soaked through all our shirts, until we had none left, so Anicka lifted off her summer dress, she lowered it over my body, it was her mother's dress, too big for her anyway. Her mother had died that year. I lay there, freezing, sweating, a dead woman's dress for a shirt. Anicka poured the wash into the tub. I want to live, I prayed like I knew how. And I was heard. Or I heard "it." The sound of shirts, flaccid, swishing, circled her hands: a nest of sexless angels.

Rue Max Jacob

A certain clock in town strikes ten minutes before the hour, then again on the hour. At dinner time the first strike calls home men who sit talking. The men nod their heads concurrently. The men wear ties. The men wear hats. It is one identical hat—a porkpie variety, jauntily set on the side of each head. And when the first strike comes the men adjust their seats a little, pause their talk, touch their jaunty hat. Then resume. Ten minutes. Now we watch the egg dance—but never crack—in boiling water.

The Skull

The mouth gulps, the brain sits and fidgets. The face in the mirror: a failed gag. You are either comically old or tragically young, it's always changing. Then a flutter of wings in the attic, or the scramble of animal feet, and the world speeds up like a silent film in which you're falling backwards, tumbling through a wind storm, your eyes wide and popping from the skull. That's what sleep is like. Get up now, draw the white curtains. It's dark outside. Senseless as you are, you left the windows open.

In Translation: Fruits and Vegetables

The days of the faithful translation are over. They came to an end with a childish prank. One afternoon at my grandmother's home in Norristown, I switched all the labels of her Depression-era stock load of peas and carrots and beets. For months she stared bereft into a freshly opened can of tubers while trying to bake a pie. Since then my sin has gone on to contaminate my life. In the morning I wake up as usual with one, almost indiscernible change . . . Today I have an upraised, very tiny, third nipple.

Max Jacob's Prayer List at Drancy

"I've forgotten no one in my continuous prayers," Max Jacob wrote the Abbot upon his reassignment at Drancy. There exist two sheets of paper covered with names, from Picasso to Jean Cocteau and many others, too, who would not have asked for his prayers. Of course, grace is not dependent on belief: it visits independent of our wishes or our need. The author of the prayer was in the gravest danger, but I've yet to find him on these lists! The writing grows tiny. Some names are just a squiggle, a mustache.

Without Adornment

The barber in his white uniform does a little dance, a little practiced step, when he turns from one side to cut its opposite. His body completes one revolution before its arrival on the Occident of your head. Your head is mostly covered, almost all the time, by your mother's spit. One self, without adornment. Your face in this mirror, the only reminder you own. All else is under the cape, which wisps a bit when he turns, and a wet lock of hair falls, square on your shoulder, and stays there gleaming like an epaulette.

Violence

Chartres is befallen with scaffolding, but no workers are
to be seen. They've constructed a bar at the altar, left there
evidence of saws and hammers. So I might be anywhere,
in any razed castle in Europe. From the windows a little
stained light willows down. Whenever the vertical turns
horizontal like this, I just feel like dancing. The bell
strikes a rondo beat. Let's order a drink, I joke, and
Anicka snaps this picture. Behind me stands a tall stoic
guide, hands at his sides, head chopped off by the frame.

The Most Natural Thing

Anicka cracked a walnut into halves and filled the halves with wax. A birthday candle in each one, she set the halves afloat, in milk. Gently she lifted the spine of the carp: it rose from the flesh in one sweeping motion. The carp lay on the table like an unbuttoned sleeve, the spine did not seem to belong there anymore. We ate the carp, the candles fizzling down. On the table was a watch, a white handkerchief. On the floor lay a doll, the eyes half opened, like hers, like mine, its painted eyebrows raised.

The Secret of Comedy

In Forman's early film, *The Fireman's Ball*, one of the guests at the ball has stolen the headcheese and will they kindly return it, once the lights are turned off? The lights are turned off. The theater goes completely black. The lights return but too quickly. The main accuser, crouched, throws like a tragic magician the cheese at the table as he dies (we're led to believe) of embarrassment. It's orchestrated too musically, too majestically, to be sad. So I laugh, because that's the way it always is, all of the time.

The Secret of Tragedy

The yellow of an apron in Vermeer describes a healthy lymph node's glow—which sometimes bloats to crabapple size, protrudes from the tree of the body. In this Vermeer, it is the milkmaid's youth, the tassel of milk, that move me to think of her death. Even the paint on the canvas is cracking, thinking of death. Because everything we see has long disappeared, it appears to deeply shine . . . The trick is to witness my own fall like that. Whatever is born must learn to grow heavy, and fall.

Removal

To feel each branching-outward part. I do not feel each part, though I have prayed to hear the small breath of my cells at Wet Mountain. The aspen grove sends messages in leaf-code to its heart, a clutch of roots. Mildew zones out in provinces. Burn up, burn up, the yellow aspen says, burn up—which is another way of saying remember who you are, as you move in your beautiful, arched-upward body, believing yourself your own kingdom, believing yourself to be only yourself, instead of the land.

Acknowledgements

Academy of American Poets 'poem-a-day': "'An Insistent and Eager Harmoniousness of Things'"

Blackbird: "'My Heart Swims in Blood'," "The Dead in Certain Old Photographs," "Take Messina," "In Translation: Woe-Mood" "In Translation: Mercury"

Colorado Review: "The Skull"

Crazyhorse: "The Crown of Light at Assisi" (pts 2 and 3), "Near the Amphitheater at Gubbio"

Dirtflask: "Aloysius Bertrand"

Descant: "The Jaw," "In Translation: 1901"

Prairie Schooner: "Whatever Sings Belongs to No one"

Ploughshares: "The Heart," "Idiom"

Florida Review: "Vasco de Gama Rounds the Horn," "In Translation: Sperm"

Nimrod: "The Most Natural Thing"

The Pinch: "The Bladder," "The Tongue"

Rosebud: "Slowness"

Washington Square: "On Seeing the Ravennan Mosaics"

Zone 3: "The Larynx"

To the Hald Hovedgaard Writers Retreat and the Danish Council on the Arts. To Hal Widener on Rue Max Jacob, St. Benoit-sur-Loire. To the National Endowment for the Arts. To friends who shepherd me through my projects: Bobbi Whalen, Amy Gussack, Kermit Moyer, Dave Singleton, Dori Sless, Dave Sless ("EP"), Colleen Morton Busch, Jen Richter, Jake Adam York, Juan Morales, Jane Hilberry, Bill Varner, Mary Koles, and Anna Carson Dewitt. To editors Bill Olsen, Kim Kolbe, Marianne Swierenga. To life-transforming mentors, Bruce Weigl, Mary Oliver, and Herb Scott.

photo by Jake Adam York

David Keplinger is the author of three books of poetry, most recently *The Clearing* (2005) and *The Prayers of Others* (New Issues, 2006), which won the 2007 Colorado Book Award. He is the recipient of an NEA fellowship, grants from the Pennsylvania Council on the Arts and the SOROS Foundation, and the T.S. Eliot Prize. In 2011 BOA, Ltd. published *House Inspections,* his translations of Danish poet Carsten René Nielsen, and in 2007 *World Cut out with Crooked Scissors,* Nielsen's selected poems, appeared from New Issues Press. Keplinger directs the MFA program in Creative Writing at American University in Washington, D.C.

The Green Rose Prize

2012: Jaswinder Bolina
       Phantom Camera

2011: Corey Marks
       The Radio Tree

2010: Seth Abramson
       Northerners

2009: Malinda Markham
       Having Cut the Sparrow's Heart

2008: Patty Seyburn
       Hilarity

2007: Jon Pineda
       The Translator's Diary

2006: Noah Eli Gordon
       A Fiddle Pulled from the Throat of a Sparrow

2005: Joan Houlihan
       The Mending Worm

2004: Hugh Seidman
       Somebody Stand Up and Sing

2003: Christine Hume   Gretchen Mattox
       Alaskaphrenia   *Buddha Box*

2002: Christopher Bursk
       Ovid at Fifteen

2001: Ruth Ellen Kocher
       When the Moon Knows You're Wandering

2000: Martha Rhodes
       Perfect Disappearance